Praise for THE CABIN AT THE END OF THE WORLD

The Cabin at the End of the World is a poignant collection delving into timeless themes of memory, dream, existence, and personal discovery. Through lyrical prose and evocative imagery, Cole navigates the landscapes of both outer travels and inner reflections, inviting readers to ponder identity and meaning against fleeting moments, the gravity of loss, and the transient nature of life, offering moments of clarity amidst the complexities of human experience.—

—**Chun Yu**, Multiple Award-winning poet; author of *Little Green,* a memoir in free verse; Library Laureate 2023 of San Francisco Public Library and an honoree of YBCA 100 award (2020) for creative changemakers and community leaders.

Douglas Cole paints with an imagist's clarity, a minimalist's precision, and a poet's sense of Duende. *The Cabin at the End of the World* is a spellbinding book which dissects and frames the fragility and intensity of the urban moment. Well done, poet!

—**Jose Hernandez Diaz**, author of *Bad Mexican, Bad American.*

"I don't mind disappearing," writes Douglas Cole in his latest collection of poems, *The Cabin at the End of the World,* and so he does, allowing his robust curiosity and lyric language to become the central players in work whose subjects run from ennui to enlightenment. Whether in poems brief and tantalizing as a Zen koan, or pieces that wend their way over many pages, Cole's unique perspectives will find readers identifying with the crab in "Winter Vision," which, having been "snatched off the beach" by a hungry crow and born aloft, receives the gift of "seeing / in a way it's never seen before."

—**Frank Paino**, winner of a 2016 Individual Excellence Award from The Ohio Arts Council, a Pushcart Prize and The Cleveland Arts Prize in Literature, he is the author of *Obscura* (Orison Books), and *Out of Eden* (Cleveland State University Poetry Center)

Douglas Cole's *The Cabin at the End of the World* is a flight through "heating ducts and beast parades" on a slowly sinking tanker, because "Who wouldn't want their illegal cargo sunk / without a trace?" This gritty and surreal book of poems is a "dusty magic phone / you can use to call your past lives." It's "Death drinking ouzo in a phone booth alone." And it's "a mariachi band / line-dancing with ghosts in the empty air." When you are done reading, walking in the post-book quiet, the darkness will swallow you and the city, and you will be whole.

      —**Scott Ferry**, author of *Sapphires on the Graves*

The Cabin
at the
End of the World

Poems by

Douglas Cole

Also by Douglas Cole

Drifter (Poetry)

The White Field (Novel)

The Blue Island (Poetry)

The Gold Tooth in the Crooked Smile of God (Poetry)

Bali Poems (Poetry)

The Dice Throwers (Poetry)

Western Dream (Poetry)

Interstate (Poetry)

Ghost (Novella)

For Jenn

"A gold-feathered bird
Sings in the palm..."
                    —Wallace Stevens

Table of Contents

The Talking Stone

The Windows of the Sea

The Cabin
at the
End of the World

Block 23

A Game of Chicken

When the train still came through town along Sand Point Way
up at the north end of the lake, we used to swing out on a rope
tied to a tree branch above the tracks in a game called Chicken,
and one boy named Stuart who was often hounded by the pack,
timid, backed away up the muddy hillside until taunted one day
he at last took hold of the frayed rope just as the engine passed,
and we watched him arc out like we had done but at the point
directly over the train he turned to face us—and what can I say
about that expression and the way it seemed like a final stab
as he let go or slipped—who could know—and was carried off,
as we scattered fast and only heard the rest of the story later
on the news but among us we never said a word about it ever.

Drive Through

He wanders up to fast food windows hoping you'll hear his confession.
A seagull flaps over his head and he rises almost hitting the ceiling fan.
He says, Mexico? Either pelicans or shamans crouch on the river rocks
with fright-night movie eyes or his own reflection in the sliding glass
as ghostly couples pass by matrimonial, transparent and wide-eyed
on the next day of the rest of their lives, as he steps out of the resort
and goes back to field basic one before the next bright idea comes along
like a pure and simple distraction in a nutshell, and he writes it down
as though he has to say stone and stone again to have anything to step on
because how else are you going to cross a road like this and how long
until you forget you're even saying road and road appears or bed or sleep
or a head to rattle around in with that sky-high primordial face up there
barely out of high school and saying snidely, so can I take your order?
And all he can think to say is, meat. I'll take the meat to go.

Revisiting Erskine Way

This was just a dirt road, and in the golden hour you still see
the dust and the outline of an old flatbed truck hauling nets
down to Lowman Beach. And where now sits this L-shaped
luxury home, there used to be a station, and now at night
if you squint, you see the shades of servicemen in overalls
going living room to kitchen, passing through your shadow.

Infinite Gaze

Darkness swallows the city down to its diamond feet and snakeskin streets,
eyes looking in, and where the theoretical equation of a black hole meets
the very real chest-crushing exhale of spirit rising like a slug from its shell,
I go into the magic bookstore, and I think I've been in these aisles before
with that smell of centuries, the fall of Rome, holy wars and blitzkriegs,
when I find that one perfect volume, slim, the only work by an obscure poet,
and here on page fourteen—either noose or loose or open window—
then I pull back another page and read the fine print and shoot through
the semiotic gap to tweak your beard and thumb my nose, here, the day
squandered without plunder and sliding away, the ship never boarded
on invisible seas portless and quarantined, cities empty this pious morn
with squabbles and busy innkeepers empire-building slow games of chess,
a space I slip through more lightly than that woman on First Avenue
who comes at you from out of nowhere tapping your forearm for change.

Mind Blank as a Room

In the street below, a woman with a chainsaw and a pick,
a child listening to a tree, thinking, why was there a split?
Old men working their asses off hauling greasy produce
boxes down the long alleyways off King Street.
It's not you that woman yells at mad as hell on 3rd and James,
a scrawny kid passed out in the crosswalk, new one arriving
fresh from the plains, windows covered with aluminum foil
shimmering like faces of fire in that hotel up above.

Pigeon Man

I come upon pigeons huddled in an alcove off Broadway—
I stop—one more bold heads right up to me—the leader,
the fearless beggar eyeing me with that dull sideways look—
I move on—I've got things to do up and down this street—
it seems like I'm going in circles—it's evening dark
when I pass that alcove again—cop cars with lights flashing,
cops on radios and cops gathered around that alcove hustling
a man in rags who looks at me as though I'm to blame—

Rolling the Bones

I've been looking through the attic vent like a wartime prisoner
you've never seen so many dead bees and the insulation smells like bacon
and you roll the bones and there's the future laid out like a news blast
and you say can't be true will never be true and go on believing it away
but the bones never lie I tell you nor the clouds nor the flight of birds
because it's all written out just like this I'm only reading the footnotes
and the subscript and I'm not even here remember I'm over here
on the other side of the sky vent though sometimes I walk beside you
or just behind you out of your line of vision listening and allowing it all
to take place and when you die I'll be standing here again but I'll put in
a good word for you to the captain because that's the least I can do

Widow Maker

I'm strolling across the Marymoor grass, high as a kite, and that music,
oh, it got me through some hairy post-party drives out of Oakland,
loading docks lit up like a gangster movie set in predawn twilight,
with razor eyes and a chippy mind, and I'm listening to your New York
infant stand-ins calling from rooftops, the moon a co-conspirator,
and when we leap from one tenement to another, covering that distance
you have to hold your breath to get the right buoyancy, and now
I'm catching your messages through heating ducts and beast parades
and random strangers who turn from other conversations and say,
Light out for the territories! Or, What are you looking at?
Going into that condemned black box high-rise, hit in the chest
by a sledgehammer wrecking ball with trickster clown at the levers,
and the irony is not lost on me as I shoot from a canon I stuffed
with cigarettes and steaks but see the view is incredible from here!

The Companion

I am traveling along the bloodstream of this building
and going down every corridor looking for the unseen
terrible heart that keeps it all going. I want to stab it
with pens and cabinet rods until dying it takes with it
that rushing black sound of the void as I step into new
spring fields of wet grass and the lush melting ice dew
soaking your legs as you move on and look and think
you see by the green eyes and the sheen of a black coat
a panther that you follow with your heart beating fast.
And I'm here waiting where you find the little black ink
spot at the back of awareness you pick at and pull open,
rending a self you believed in in the process, the moment
so much like a death but realizing you're just being born.

The Couple in Room 416

She said, you seem like you're acting.
After this long, he said, of course you see the strings.
But that's what we do for each other, isn't it?
Allow a show the other worked so hard to create:
this grand self, this charlatan, this ghoulishly got-up
spectacle of character laughing in the funhouse,
a mechanism pantomiming speech, love, a virtual self.

But you look so real,
she kept saying,
you look so real.

Backwards Revolved the Luminous Wheel

I got your book in French. I don't read French, but I'm Tarzaning the Latin roots
and bushwhacking my way through like a temple explorer, a Naturalist in the wild—
cataloguing as I go. I know, I should be working. I'm in a lull, you see? Somewhere
between the Buddha garden and the wine dark sea. I know you hate pretentious shit,
empty boxes, armies of workers clearing out your recycling as punishment, strictly as
punishment for what the haze-maker can do. What's the value of a diamond now
except for its flaws? Something's so retro-beaux arts steampunk in a Chitty Chitty
Bang Bang sort of way about these glasses and your laughter, it's like you've grown
into that Empire chair, your body at least. What you'd call your brain is hanging from
a hook-light in the garage with drills and bandsaws. Explains the million-mile stare.
But your book! Your book! I see you in there character slumming, running lines,
hovering between the period and the scene. These glasses are amazing. Neither snow
nor sleet nor dark of night, time, distance, death—I've made a few heavens myself.
In fact, I'm in Zone Eight now. What can I say? I love the undulations, the footnotes,
the biographical and historical references. Even the symbol of the blue heron
turning into a lighthouse: that was pure genius. I always knew you had it in you.

The Street of Lost Steps

Jim Carroll hits the west coast, his visions fueled by quitting junk.
He's on the methadone plan, says he's becoming an "anti-social hermit."
This is fifty years before Patti Smith conjures *Year of the Monkey*. Same coast.
Yet her scene arrives unannounced in a whisper from the Dream Motel.
She's in the west but moving in and out of time like a migrating butterfly.
Cross-fertilize this with Jim Harrison and Charles Simic (*Dime Store Alchemy*),
with one of them, not Carroll, mentioning hermits—not the anti-social kind.
In fact, that's underlined, though without a reference, and seems like the key.
Find them and put them all together, then you might know what's coming:
an anti-social hermit or a dazzling, mysterious monk in exquisite reclusion.

Ivan

There's a man called Ivan going through these opening cartoon doors,
mid-March with some anniversary in the back of his mind he's forgetting,
sliding by pampas grass in waist-high vases the woman brought from Padilla Bay
with their silvery feelers floating off and clinging to the outline he just left,
as he plows into mountains of air shaped like The Brothers, and he's my other,
slogging through court cases, church services, branch meetings, subway rides,
burials and bewildering resurrections, closing a book on a finger and looking up
as if he just heard something, that outline still hanging in the air before him.

No SOS On

I was going to lunge back for something in the car, but by then the car had vanished.
These things happen, you know, when a crow shuffles its wings and strops its beak
on a powerline over the city with record temperatures and a big freighter leaning
or listing rather dangerously in the bay. Who wouldn't want their illegal cargo sunk
without a trace? Or proclaim the wriggling newborns are hungry and innocent?
And who would imagine the moment those nasty memories start floating up again
and the look on the face? I'm navigating subtle waters and mist, which is to say
I have no manifest nor customs nor pirate flag. Nothing incandescent about this,
code it as you may, flopping around with psychedelic horns and spurs—you catch
only a glimpse of what I'm up against, which you will be up against soon enough.
All I can say is practice practice practice—knowing you ride a breath is the ticket
to riding it away, meaning I'm in no hurry to return to harbor or your regulations,
with all these possibilities, no agenda, nothing separating me from the high seas.

Notes for The Grey Man

He's in the woods somewhere down a trail off the main trail and down through
stickers and ferns in a cedar grove where he sees out but no one can see in.
Some of these fallen trees, the hollow rotting ones, if you touch them you feel
the vibrations of hikers in the distance. I feel him listening with his hands,
a spider picking up our trembling movement in its invisible web.

Because from the elbow of 56th and Manning you can see Bainbridge Island,
the green hills of Winslow, and further on Indianola, the other side of the sound,
out-jut of Magnolia, and there, that's Whidbey. I think that's Whidbey Island,
Useless Bay...out...the mind travels over it and out.

The God tree on Spokane and 59th curves to the edge of sky. Buildings on sticks
launch west from Cormorant Cove, each apartment with its own glass balcony,
waves rolling in, an altar on the shoreline with roaches and vials. And 65th
between Stevens and Admiral is a time warp because it's below sea level,
with shanty-style slant-roof A-frames, with cordwood stacked on porches,
boat trailers covered in green sea-muck, and a few steps more, a grotto home
with Seuss trees, blue-lit hedges and gardens, glowing lead-lined windows,
and a horseshoe driveway so far back you can barely see that vivid
primitive kid on a bicycle riding around and around in a figure eight.

At Wilton Court where only warm wind, jasmine and lavender take a stand
under the streetlamp, someone's got a barbecue going, a party, smoke and laughter
rolling into Bar S Field...a corner of paradise evaporating like spit on a hot sidewalk.
And Glad Harbor, at the end of the strip, is a Hollywood house with ceiling-to-floor
windows wrapped around and looking over the point, the ghost of Frank Sinatra
smoking on the sunset patio with fountains trickling away, and a woman
walking right through his crooning outline with her summer robe full of sea air.

The lighthouse, nautical Blue Dolphin, bamboo growing up the spiral staircase,
and that ramshackle place down the gravel drive, again, something once elegant
now element-worn, coming apart, I stumbled one night from the Celtic Swell
with some new friends, saying, "Ever notice those high-tone flat-bottom clouds
slow-sliding across the sky, but when you look...when you really look...you see

big heavies and fringes and thin sheens like slips of paper all going different speeds,
different directions, some barely moving because wind is multidirectional,
currents and crosscurrents, eddies and still spots—I'm wondering how it fractal-like
resembles other systems, real or theoretical…I mean, water…time…a life…"
watching a couple on their couch going at it, a Road Runner cartoon on the TV,
and did it just say Looney Tunes or Looney Toons? I can't remember.

Some mornings, most mornings, wake up, and everything feels different.
Rearrangement, a few missing pieces, things there that weren't there before,
the commentator typing…continuity error…I push through this with black
spiders at the edge of things disappearing if you look directly at them,
showing up when you look away, weaving the dream fabric as they go.

Ride into the self like a baffling professor on a long plane flight, going on
about the real writer of Shakespeare's works, and then a drone-dead sky
blasted open with no parachute to cling to, orange fuzz growing from my hands,
eyes in all directions, a vibrating deep in the head, rafters creaking, earthquake,
big winds and needling, ground-emulsifying rain…let's see you watch your face
dissolve down to the letters, then join me at the corner pocket, drinking till three,
a good run going on the pool table. I saw every shot before it happened.

When I went to bed I spun for a while without center and ended up here,
and I tell you I finally get it after all those shots how you can sink a life
and rise from the wreckage with those friends stuck in the butterfly wake,
white snakes burning in a ditch of fire, glide over a still lake with no shadow
and live to tell about it in a way no one expects, even if they're not surprised.

American Dharma

Winter Vision

Sitting in a thin ray of sunlight
midwinter still neither warm nor cold
the blue bell of sky ringing out
a crow taking off with a crab
that it snatched off the beach
the crab now dangling and seeing
in a way it's never seen before

Eternity Bookstore

Cockeyed shelves, out-of-print books,
gadgets and rubber eyes,
glow-in-the-dark skeletons
and a dusty magic phone
you can use to call your past lives.

The Beauty of the World

Death drinks ouzo in a booth alone.
Death checks names in a ledger book.
Death punches A2 on an old jukebox
and plays a Buddy Holly tune.
Death caresses your Christmas tree.
Death rides the bus and sits in back
whispering Hamlet's soliloquy.
Death floats down the alleyway
in smoke from a neighbor's chimney.
Death drains off your boozy eggnog
and hovers somewhere in the wings.
Death watches your every move.
Death sends regards in a dream,
in a cough, in a sleepless night,
in a phone call, a piece of mail,
a light bulb you tap that comes to life.

Boethius Said

The butcher spends his life in blood and guts,
      the professor in his books.
When their cities flood, fire ants band together
      on floating islands of the dead.
I am stepping from the mountain top
      into chest-sinking freedom.
I hear someone saying in disbelief,
      Should be snuffed out for good!
As I slide on shoes of light and stroll
      with my hands behind my back.

On Broadway

You quit smoking. You lost your ID,
       all your money, accounts wiped clean—
that feeling, that moment walking down the street
       patting your pockets, realizing you have nothing,
are nothing, with no one looking for you,
       and the tag on your toe says John Doe.
Yes, I'm speaking to you, the only one who sees you
       in your coat of cloud and freedom blush.

Flowmatic

Satoshi Kon says, where are you going?
Everyone is walking around in their bones.
The fish woman prays to the moon,
or Manu's bodega, and that stomachache
is the roller coaster rising and falling
in the tunnel where anything can happen.
Satoshi Kon says, look, and re-draws
passenger faces on the water taxi
that hover, shudder and don't quite fit
the oval of the skull, and he says,
this is just a reminder, as I look down
and see that I'm all lines and spaces.
Satoshi Kon says, face mirror to mirror
and you'll get an infinite reaction.
Satoshi Kon says, put these two together
and then we'll see what happens,
re-draw skyline, flip night into day.
I say, wait, wait as backdrops roll away.
Satoshi Kon hands me a pen—his words
floating in a bubble over his head—
draw your way out if you want or in,
as a freight truck guns it up Yesler Way.

The Messenger

A man stands facing oncoming wind and everything it drags with it,
and he knows, this man, that he will never be rich, he will never swim
to the edge of an infinity pool with the sun setting so warm and close
he could put his hand out and feel it travel into his closing fingers
and believe he carries it and all its chaos and heat and power in his fist,
that image that dissolves into a true aging face as he tells the same joke
or the same story to a new set of strangers in a cool, badly lit room,
people still believing behind their smiles of gratitude that they too,
because they've taken this first step, might be closer to their own
private palaces, even hoping, if they're lucky, they might be able
to push a child or two up that mountain of fog called success,
and just maybe, if they're lucky or pray to the right god, that child
might turn and pull them along, offering a room or an allowance
or some other access to luxury and food—comfort as a base to drift
and meditate and perfect the soul—all this unspoken, unexamined
yet going on as the man in the front of the room stops and stares,
with his story having reached its message-bearing conclusion,
lifts his hand and presses it below his throat, heart beating fast,
eyes wide as he remembers something important he forgot to say.

Dear Reader

The secret door through which we come and go
in the shape of an almond at the back of the head,
appears from time to time in theaters, schools,
churches, buildings you want to call home,
and on that rusty junker left in the damp grass,
as you stand slightly apart, there, and I take you
like a thrown kiss and press you into my chest
where your ghostly fingers curl like a prisoner's
around the bars of ribs that glow like rays of light.

Lashed to the Mast

He says, "I'm the best…" if you can believe it,
in his big-chest, beach-side gumba talk—
as the flood waters rise and he throws back a shot
and puts up his fists and says, "I'll take all of you on,"
as if that makes a true living piece, a mystery smile
we puzzle over in the void of a ferry run to the island,
a navel-gazing sunroom where attendants shuffle
what's left of the monster in, and still we recoil,
even if he's lost his teeth. "Just wait, just wait,"
he says, "I'll get you in the next round!"

Into the Zone

We go deeper and deeper into the building.
People wear smocks and masks. Corridors are dim.
Overhead lights flicker, sounds of voices, moans,
overlapping streams of music. An aid pushes a gurney
with a body on it covered by a sheet. I hear buzzing.
Someone asks for directions to the department of…what,
I couldn't hear with that muffled mouth, but I nod—yes,
yes, and point down the hallway to the left.

Dead Center

Somewhere, an old man is sitting in his dim cabin
trying to make out these words. Did I write this?
He wonders, fire crackling, as ideas leap off the page.
And he's free, now, of all that worry and the weight
that gets measured at the official border, the kind of thing
you pat your coat pockets for, saying, now where did I...
as the checkpoint guard shakes his head and rolls his eyes.

Body of Evidence

Sound of a baby crying, very faint but very clear,
crickets showing up dead on the back porch,
as if dropped from sky or blown in from the West.
Something's out of alignment, but what and how to fix it?
I'm dreaming only in Spanish: me destino es entrar
con alegria este earopuerto. We are only sound after all.
La luna illumina la noche. I like to say it then it's true.
Faces come out of the walls saying, this way, or how are you?
Bamboo windchimes not far off, can paradise be close behind?

Double Tree

A vague, grey, Eastern European darkness,
though it really should be light by now.
The remote isn't working, not even a blink.
When I peek through the door, not a soul.
Patterns in the carpet change every glance—
from Aztec to Gaelic to Corinthian—like
I'm standing on an architectural blueprint,
between shifting smiles and question marks.
This coffee doesn't seem to be doing the trick.

Sit-ups, push-ups, anything to move the blood.
Frosted mirrors bubble like eggs in a skillet.
It takes forever just to cross the room,
open a window to its suicide-preventing limit:
gaze on black tar roof below, a lake beyond that,
and through the trees a sound like engines,
construction, or breathing slow in a dream.

As I head down the telescoping hallway,
all this has the smooth confusion of a birth.
The word Infinity appears as if written
on every identical door and the bland artwork,
while I'm tipping and turning as though below
deck on a ship, my own inner ear tuned in
to a mysterious frequency—a mariachi band
line-dancing with ghosts in the empty air.

Stop. The floor sinks like flesh as I reach
for vanishing door handles, stairways of light,
the commanding green emergency exit signs,
and so much distance I'm surprised, shaking
my head as I say, wait, I know this place,
rising through cloud-rippling hotel sheets.

Four Way

The past is a foggy boat ride to Riverside.
The present is a black cloud of birds in flight.
The future is music from a Chinese restaurant.
And I'm a signal operator and lighthouse keeper
in that movie full of unknowns you still remember.

Casino People

The Angel of the Winds and heat devils rise on a highway
going nowhere. And there, a fallen farmhouse crushed as though
sky pushed down from above and ground pushed up from below,
timbers snapping, souls like swallows bursting through the doors—

Out here people call property a spread, and a horse is a true identity.
Most run machine shops, drive truck, or receive disability yet say
they work the land, wear cowboy boots and jeans, give you Jack and Coke
when you're seventeen and don't bat an eye when you start smoking.
They're not religious, but if you aren't Christian you're suspicious.

They want homes set back from the road with room for goats, guns,
new tires, and a new transmission, a local bar to watch the game in,
a solid retirement or government pension and good television reception.
They respect the man with a clean haircut and a straight stack of wood,
make it part of birthday celebrations to burn the back field brush
and float down river on inner tubes with coolers full of cans of beer,
follow high school sports to see who punches through to the big leagues,
sneer down those who leave and shake their heads at those who never go,
break out snow tires and chains in winter, respect the cocktail hour,
watch black and white movies for cultural history, play Tammy Wynette,
Waylon Jennings, drive pick-ups and get tattoos of Jesus on their biceps.

Too much, no way you say, that all sounds like sad stereotypes,
but I know, I live among them: Uncle Billy with a big gut he'd slap
and call his investment went out fast by heart attack at forty-eight.
Gentry made it to nearly seventy, but after a lifetime of cigarettes
and exposure to asbestos from his time in the navy, he got cancer.
The worst thing, he said at the end, were the constant hiccups.

Hard by thirty with relentless debt, foreclosures, lost weekends
in roadside motels or the Big Lake cabins, savings gambled away…

We go down a misty backroad, crazy Joe waving at the headlights,
and he's saying, never be in a hurry and you'll always be on time,
as meadowlarks come alive and The Angel of the Winds arrives,
lifting the broken bones of a farmhouse in a swirl of swallows,
earth pushing up, something else pushing down from the sky.

The Talking Stone

Road of Bones

Look up ahead, black road going back
through the white hills, fields fading out
into rolling mist...a dream, a buried past,
something surging to the surface:
broken mud planks in the mining camp,
barbed wire, the hump of a gravesite—
you can drive forever and never see
another soul, and eventually the road
itself disappears into a snowbank.

The Desert Motel

You couldn't have picked a better place to evaporate.
Nothing in the icemaker, every direction you turn
hot wind with grit and bone particles, sigh and outlines
once human midway journey up a stack of steer skulls,
equally into green water in a half-empty swimming pool.
Somehow still a balance. When you leave the world
you're in the world that much more. A sticky proposition,
toying with dream. One muddy truck in the parking lot,
sign faded to 'go away,' road under creeping sand and this
hole we tunnel into, shadows passing over the wolf moon
like intermittent signals from an abandoned weather station
where a book leaning against a keyboard is tapping out
its undying messages triggered by nothing but the wind.

Getting Yourself Home

I'm walking home from Charlie and Yumi's house
after one, mist is sliding through the live oak trees
as I'm figuring out the geometry involved in a point
where Virginia Street and Euclid Avenue meet.
Orange filaments glow from my hands, sight extends
in all directions. Can you imagine how quiet it is?
The surprise when a police car appears, window down,
and a cop says, "You hear anyone scream out here?"
How is he so calm with caterpillars crawling on his face?
Imagine a powerlifter doing a clean-and-jerk, bar loaded
to twice his weight and you might get an idea just what
it takes for me to open my mouth and say, "No."
The patrol car slithers off, blue light burning a trail
that feels like static electricity as I pass through it.

Patrolman

Highway patrolman on his stretch of road
snaking through the green-black forest
goes back and forth between two towns
and some days forgets which is which,
the road like a flat river in summer
rolling from sea to shining sea,
and once in a while when he's bored
he drives off into one of those fields alone
there on his Mobius strip where he knows
every gravel bit by name, each drop-off
and all the hollows and the overpasses,
the trunks and tires and shirts he finds,
a dresser drawer and once a human skull,
abandoned cars and wandering people lost,
the road his road his world his place,
he could get away with murder out here
and thinks of it long hours going round
as he hits the lights to pull you over.

Tuesday's Purge

The white droning of a shredder truck
at someone's garage, box tops flipped open,
gloved hands shoveling documents
into the orange baleen, not a puff of dust,
and your stuff is gone. You stand there clean
as if you never existed, truck moving off
fiber-heavy with the debris of you.
Your head fills up with possibilities.

The End of the World

The end of the dream will be bright
angels descending in golden columns
through the smoky industrial night,
turning into airplanes approaching a field,
as the grey-clad officials board their long
dark buses with windows tinted black,
and police cordons hold the traffic back
as they go into the compounds of the city,

through the underground networks,
secret tunnels, to arrive at the nerve center
with convoys loaded with the last food,
while outside hunger-maddened, disposable
people hurl themselves against razor wire,
trying to get a few crumbs from the masters.

Circular Highway

Not far out of the city you'll find the billboard
with Uncle Sam and some bible verses on it,
an old power plant, a town where you might disappear
and nobody investigate, faces behind screen doors,
the sound of gameshows in living rooms,
and you'll barter for food and dry firewood,
a burial suit, with secret signs on the water tower,
the past loading up in the second-hand store,
technology that doesn't work, books, luggage,
worn shoes with the shape of feet still in them
you take from the shelf with a flash of the life
that walked before now passing through you,
standing by an abandoned truck, leaning in grass,
the evening whispering through corn stalks
in a field you enter with a rush of relief.

Healing Rain

Bury him deep boys,
and throw lye on the bones.
We want nothing left,
nothing ever found, not one
code, not one stitch to reanimate,
all of it gone, and you, boy,
I didn't catch your name—
wipe that smile off your face.

Chasing Tiger

You're porch surfing on a futon
with a few books on a handmade shelf,
guitar, Hawaiian shirt, gig at a coffee shop,
a short story about your younger self.
You light up nights you have the place
to yourself, ranting King Richard:
"Dog, I will strike thee to my foot!"
Mining the words for hidden fuel,
singing, "Should I Stay or Should I Go,"
in post-war stance, fight and flight skin,
an edgy mushroom dilated glare
with October rippling like curtains
into a fight with the brother and sister,
girl you brought back now heading down
the stairs, sky splitting primal, the Duster
with bald tires and pollen on the windshield,
you behind the wheel going to the big frontier
back north and roads you dissolve into,
Navy recruit photo on the rearview mirror
fluttering with the incoming wind,
cattleguard vibrating your bones as you pass
into the open fields between nations.

Caught in a Dream

Woke up in the middle of the night in the middle of a windstorm,
saw all the homes were dark, power out in our part of the city,
black cubes, black rooftops and the black sea, and I thought a moment
something critical had happened, a catastrophe, war, meteor, virus.
I thought some big damage had been done, still fresh from dream
with dream thoughts, like, look for survivors, assess damage, get water.
You see, the wind was still delivering a right cross and an uppercut,
things in motion that were typically still. Darkness. How to describe it?
Like an abandoned theater, as I wander through the empty rooms
because there's no one else here. Time is happening without me.
I put my hands on the cold window, breath turning white on the glass,
as I say into my own face there, Wake up! Wake up!

Cartoon Moment

The insane window washer is
trying to scrub his reflection out,
sees death leering back at him
from the other side of transparency.
The spider swings on a single thread
looking for a place to put the moon.
The washer leans back on the ladder,
falling slowly with flailing arms
into the pillow-crash of a green lawn
as the streets, trees, faces in doorways
follow his body-hole into the ground.
And I rise from these opening eyes
that I loaned you with surplus care
and reenter the swirling chaotic air.

Lonesome Driver

I feel like I'm driving forever—at every stop
lifetimes slam up against the back of my head—
even you float by in a doppler wave
bending into a siren wail in the dark—
and around midnight just when I find a station
on the motel TV, a hard knock comes at the door
and a child standing there with a pamphlet asking
where will you be at the end of the world.

Estrella

That kid shows up in jeans and t-shirt
panther-walking Normal Heights,
dreaming *Pedro Paramo* and *Macario*
in a cool theater chapel in the desert,
rows of stucco homes on Adams Avenue,
church bells ringing in the canyon,
cat demons lurking in the courtyard,
crazy apartment manager in the alleyway
screaming, "I'll burn the place down!"

Dark Carnival

I use your business cards as bookmarks—that way you ride with me for sure.
Let someone else explain the equation of that without confusing heart, matter,
spirit and thought. On page seventy-three, the cloud parts, and there's the door
to your magic shop, the mystery telephone on an upper shelf—call any time,
call the dead, you can call yourself in another head—ugly dolls, tarot packs,
glow-in-the-dark skeletons, a safe space for the off-kid in the dusty aisle
patting his shoulders and mumbling his locker combination and on occasion
pieces of particle theory he heard in a documentary. There's always access,
new volumes, old tomes stacked high and rare collectibles in the back
rooms I haven't the lives to explore going off and more additions on the way.
Everything from science fiction, esoterica, philosophy and good old standards,
even *The Gold Tooth* and more coming, and you, homuncular in your bric-a-brac,
still sullen and distant but with a glint of never-ending wonder in your eye.

Distances

I wave hello to my neighbor in his hut…hello neighbor. It's quiet out
here on the peninsula. Hardly see a soul. Be still, retreat, isolate down
to the fraught night. The rich have fled to their homes in the country.

And when I drive, the roads are nearly empty. Hardly a plane goes by.
Black spots in the cityscape where industry lights used to be. I drive
to the south end across the river. Everything seems grey, blue-grey.

And out there, a barely discernible island. Wave to the woman high
on the list. Catch the scent of ocean. An empty road, empty baseball
field, springtime blossom. The ones who live are the ones who move.

You forget, and that's your blessing. The low tide slides out, and shore
rocks glisten. Waves talk in the language of hiss. You forget who
you are in the big reveal. Look me in the eye, gull, show me your bliss.

Twice now I've driven down First Avenue and seen the same train
coming north, same triple headlights, same brakeman swinging
from the last car to hunt down stragglers looking to ride free.

There's no wind to speak of, so these kids will never launch their kite.
The air and the water tremble with a digital glitch. It's a simulation
walking from here to there. It's a triangle that looks a lot like a square.

It's a rendition of street names that code to the past. It's a gym
basement with weights and gloves made by Everlast. Try it again,
try every sickening step, every school, all the ten thousand versions.

An angel whispered into my ear. Wave yourself on. Wave to the smoke-
borne souls. Wave to the ghost in the mirror, on the deck of the boat.
Wave to the man in Muslim robes. Wave to the one you are up ahead.

Wave at the fly that lands in your beer. Wave it away. Wave like you
mean it. Like it matters. And don't hold your breath. Wave in
arriving stars, the dark, your fear. An angel whispered into my ear.

Again, it came on ships. Hands and faces pressed to portholes.
No land will take them. Dead overboard and dead in the hold.
Go away, go away…music and voices coming over the water.

And then it arrives. How did you get in here? The supervillain turns
into smoke and slides through keyholes, through open windows,
through half-cracked doors and the speaker holes in your phone.

Nobody move. No one leaves the city. You arrived mid-March or
earlier, lying low and hiding. How much *Bonanza* have we binge-
watched? I really can't drink like that anymore. What a blackout.

You see there's a wire that runs through my eye and that fake banana-
flavored medicine that didn't work, that time on Benvenue I melted
windows with fever touch (I still have hearing loss from that one).

Numbers rising. Stay put. Even in your head. Drink hot liquids. Focus
on the ceiling crack. See the split, golden light pouring through?
Don't you want it? Don't you want to pick at the plaster and let it in?

Strange night broadcast. Who's in charge of the station? Anyone?
Voices. We are voices in the void. I bet ten thousand quatloos
they can't be trained. Change the channel! I've seen this one already.

Watched *After Hours, World's End, Snatch*, comedy routines, *Russian
Doll, Philadelphia Story, It's a Wonderful Life, Apocalypse Now,
Sherlock Holmes, Sunset Boulevard, 8½, 400 Blows, Pedro Paramo.*

I've got the theater all to myself. I can watch all night. I can drive down
Fifth Avenue at seventy five. I can stand on the pier block here,
seagulls clustering, bell buoys ringing, the ship out there still circling.

Hazy night. Is this illegal? I tell you this guy has the good stuff. Dogs
barking in back yards. Let's go. Why even try? He's got a sponge mat
outside his door soaked in bleach. He calls it the sole disinfection area.

Hit him with the raygun! Does he check out? Yeah, he seems okay.
Hot red paper lanterns. Rainwater in pools on the black cement.
Is that all there is? Cause if that's all there is. Then try the pangolin.

A truck waiting. Sometimes I'm just suddenly somewhere else.
Tent flap back, still under the moon. Silver plain, middle of nowhere.
Pack it all up. We'll head that way. Light in the haze, blue, blue-grey.

A man appears. What, hey, where are you coming from? Blaine,
I was in Blaine. You came all this way on foot? On my old reliables!
You're on this road alone? How do you think I made it this far?

And back that way, where you come from? Rough, he said. They have
the sickness there. And beyond that? The same. It's all the same.
And where you come from? he asked. I said, there, too, the same.

Everything seems grey, blue-grey. Sad professor in the alleyway.
Sad professor at the door of the cabaret, waiting for the blue angel.
Sad professor with papers on Melville, Aquinas, and de Tocqueville.

A lightbulb, an egg, an inspiration. Wake up! Wake up! Change
the channel. Isolation chamber, altered state, magician in a box
making a miraculous bus escape on that one-lane mountain road.

Everything is grey, blue-grey. Triple headlights coming, yard bull
jumping at the slow turn, Doyle looking down from a pullman car,
Kinglsey in the mist. We are in new relations with the unseen.

Quiet dark night, I am sitting in the dim-lit kitchen, back door open,
no sound from the world but gentle rain, gate locked. Is that the ocean
or an explosion? White fire of a star magnolia in the grey, blue-grey.

Our dreams keep us alive. The spirit of Yaa may just grant your wish.
The transient ringing tinnitus. The distressed crying bird. The Imaginos.
The kingdom of mist, fly buzzing in a room, ship horn in the distance.

See the festive lights above the cliffs? Hear the music? Come. Come
to our electric circus. What have you got to lose? Go into the belly
of the beast. Retreat. Smoke. Study McKenna on language. Listen.

From the back porch I stretch these arms across the liquid sky.
Language talks. Falling stars pop on your skin. You're an angel
on the head of a pin. Hear what I'm saying, says the informing voice.

Imagine someone behind everything you see saying light, saying cloud
shaped like a whale, saying thin poplar branches, rooftop, sleeping dog,
Matthew's Beach, and the train coming 'round the north end of the lake.

While you're at it, imagine a voice like your own voice saying
everything you remember, saying what you read in a voice rising
from the printed page, asking, is this the face before you were born?

Do you like it here at the center of your own disorder? I'm restless.
Always been restless. I drive and drive and get nowhere, every day.
I sit in one room. I sit in another. Once, I made myself presentable.

I wash my face. I make food. I look out a window. Time is very slow.
Winter extends itself. I lift weights, think and read. Spring is under
glass. And if you read much further, you become part of the fable.

And that sound? Caveat lector. Hear it? That sound inside your head?
That tone? I think you can touch it. Lapiz in hand, the wave, because
I've always heard that being a little beat-up is a normal way of life.

I keep thinking something wonderful is about to happen. I hear
"And She Was," a ghost-goddess in the illness air. Like stepping out
of the shower, cool morning, steam coiling, blooming, we are mist.

Looking inward on a swampy day, the first self, the flower of Abaddon,
something moving just below the surface of the skin. I try to push it out
through the black hole where it got in, its tail slithering down my arm.

Heat. Heat and hot drinks. Keep moving. Kill it. Keep moving. Keep
temperature up. Kill it with heat. Fly into the sun. Ahhhh. Settle down.
Let it pass. Stay open inside terror. We each have our own observer.

Eat an edible. Continue "Theory and Practice of Rivers." Sleep when
needed. Watch documentaries on New York. Speak as little as possible.
Say goodbye to Max Von Sydow. Mind-read an old stack of journals.

Imagine you are the artisan. Is the world ready for the new work?
Wish well to children who want their stories spoon-fed. Enjoy
your mystery. Read. Thoughts settling like dust in an empty room.

Stare at the wall in a fever dream rolling with all its hidden things.
Keep your head to the south. Spot the roman à clef like this,
a where's waldo of prestidigitation. Follow random electronic leads.

Mystery theater, flea play, boy under water. The signal hiccups come,
look the other way. So dependent on air. Sit through the windstorm.
Sit through the rain, the gentle rain. Sleepless night. Walls of flame.

When the drugs wear off, feel the poison smoke, the sleeping body
near, lives lived and lost, ripples on the surface. Spirit is bombarded
by thinking: one who constructs the maze and then is lost within it.

Slide into the deep rhythm. Come up for air. Press through the door.
Smell the beach fires. A man walks the beachside park. I've never
seen him before. When he passes, grass blackens and flowers curl.

The tanker circles the harbor but never lands. Crows move on.
Many of our old ones are gone. The gull says, come on, come on.
A ringing in the ears. Disequilibrium. Days that feel like a dream.

This is raw data from the epicenter. Day zero. Wave zero. Who dares
appear at the masquerade dressed like that? Count backwards
from one hundred. Tides rising higher. The cure is a message in code.

Women dressed as death pass by, and as their fingers brush my chest
I feel a rise. Knock or none I hear knocking, music from another room
when there is no other room. Man in a boat offers fish to the moon bear.

I am walking through walls, yards, glittering streets and dead ends,
through squatter camps to the steps down to the alleyway and out
through the grey, through spitting rain, the spray of caustic waves.

I bushwhacked my way into *The Lost Son*, then on into *The Brothers*.
I chiseled away at *The Bright Angel*. *The White Field* was born in
a flash. Put them here, lash them together like a raft to float away on.

Hike up over Duwamish Head, then down to the sound to the mouth
of the river. Is somebody following me? Shake it off. Seems like another
normal day. Can't tell if those are gulls or buzzards circling up above.

The dead walk in our shadows, and then they walk up ahead. Here come
the fierce invalids. It's in the air, so there's nothing you can do about it.
Make no mistake. Post-war asbestos houses shimmer on the sunset hill.

Lobster metaphysics, a grain of sand, the center of a nesting doll, a black
hole, heads or tails, quantity null, void, void, nothing, never was yet still,
then what good are words like "future" or "past" in this constant instant?

I am walking through an open desert, a coastline field, a trail into a red
canyon, and down through the sun-blasted, searing, keening, canyon
silence where everything old is new, everywhere, and then the sea again.

The mother falls sick, and the sickness enters the land, enters us all.
Pray, pray for the mother, arrive with your dreams like the cavalry,
drivers refusing to enter the city, barricades, patrols, searchlights, pray.

Keep the fire going, throw everything we have in the pot, cook it up.
Count backwards from one hundred. Who parked that hearse out front?
Ninety-nine, ninety-eight, ninety-seven, this way through mystery air.

People and places lose their charm, the clouds float so low you can
almost touch them. Touching a person is like touching a cloud. Listen
to the shift-creak of the house around you. Every room is empty space.

Ninety-six, ninety-five, ninety-four, feels like we've been here before.
Bass-beat from the luxury liner, glimpse of shadowless things on deck.
Ninety-three, ninety-two, cellars deep enough to get us through.

The master investigator spots the connections. Everything is a clue.
Scrutiny reveals parts of a larger case. Victorian domes o'erlooking
the sea. What do the clouds say? We've always known everything.

The Windows of the Sea

West Cove

I

Cabin in darkness, when I rise the world's not yet invented.
I start a fire, make coffee, feel rain in the air over the porch,
gaze where not a star is born from years eaten by a factory,
time lost in traffic, time lost in a corner bar, people I know
though I don't know their names come for the same reasons,
and I'm stripping house shingles to burn through winter.

Now is a west-looking face, cherry tree humming with insects.
Thousands of years bees cycle in and out of the spring air,
Emerge, disappear then they're here again as if a voice said
be and they are as crows drop to shore and fold their wings,
become quiet monks wandering the cove in their black robes.

Gulls rise and circle out and then return as if to say, see,
you thought we were leaving but we've only just arrived.
The geese have the power to project their horn-honks out
to the far side of the cove as they fly off in other voices.
And the sound mirrors the sky-blue sky full of caravans,
kingdoms and empires in the shape of temporary clouds.

Where the tractor has left a deep scar in the sand
the old man shuffles in obsessive dance to heal it.
I keep looking out the window but checking for what?
Something's not right about that gardener.
It's too still out here. The island, the slow rolling water,
almost all black cards when I deal out solitaire.

II

Along the cove at night, with smell of wood stove fires,
darkness opens up, Orion over Flattop Island, a quiet
that makes your head explode and disappear again.
Re-entry, absurd storm, rooftops littered with cedar limbs,
dream a road and road appears, a country store with pelts
and shotguns, camp goods, a rattlesnake floating in a jar,
a door slamming on a porch as you say, there you are.
Nothing doing, we make love in the wood panel room
with the sound of the tide sliding over the rocks
and under the floorboards, crosscurrents and gull cries,
and that musical crackling of the fire at sunrise.

East Sound, no one's actively looking for me now,
ten removes from a radioactive name, with an old truck,
old home on a quiet lane on an island so small no lights
on the roads, night dark as nothing, so silent you'd say
that's what silence should look like, days I never talk,
never see another soul, my place so far from the road
if someone comes it must mean trouble, so I drift light,
and the tide flats fill and drain, old man out collecting
driftwood, pulling his two-handle cart through the rain.

At Olga's graves I catch the sign in the rearview mirror,
off paved onto gravel road, homes apart in the hills,
stacks of cordwood, chimney smoke and birch trees,
the dead extend from granite tablets in rope enclosures,
back to born in 1863, the war dead, the infants dead,
uneven ground around, subterranean fields and caves,
the scattered few, mist assembly, the stone remembers:
here, put your ear to its cold cheek and listen.

Cocktail hour, five o'clock…oh, the generations back,
decanters and pipe smoke, some crooner on the radio,
a deer over the hood of a car and a drink at end of day,
water bright with sunset light, play a song on the guitar,

read a little more Li Po, Wang Wei, then bury the mind
under waves before you decide to come up for air again.
Coming and going of itself, so quiet in fact you might hear
Octavia's bell calling all the tent campers to dinner.
Ferry at anchor, swaying back and forth in the cool moonlight,
and this great island, dark enigma in the deep black night.
How long I've only seen through the chink of weak eyes.

III

The road no one goes down to my cabin under moss,
half-buried in the hillside, old world fog rolling through—
it takes incredible patience to know how each drop of rain
cuts away another layer, and water can tell how it took down
mountains to liberate you—can you imagine it? Weight gone?
Leaves tremble from invisible storms, limbs whip empty air,
and all the thought that brought us here shimmers in mist,
something to escape far behind, and winter opens a heavy door,
entering the good warm room, surveys the option on forever.

Night like a prayer at the end of the cove—end of the world,
there is a darkness and a silence that is pure home.
Here the spirit enters itself, saying this is where I come from,
this is where I belong. The mind looking on at this says
bless me with your depth your beauty and your grace.
Talking to yourself, your mind's still a-chatter with all
those attachments, the grind of the engine, the road
that brought you here. I'm saying keep the fire going
even as tides come in. I'm not waiting for an answer,
playing solitaire again like a gangster on the lam, a ghost
breathing in the walls, asking, what do you have to return to?
You might think, yeah, and lay down another card.
My grandmother burned through thousands of decks,
wearing off the numbers and the faces, going blind until
the game was just a way to keep her hands busy.

Standing on the water, night comes in and makes its claim,
a hawk in flight with last light on its wings, the dog asleep
with muddy paws twitching in a hunt dream.
Reading a book in the darkening room, slipping into sleep,
the world is gone, now complete, nothing but a frequency
so thin, so faint that not even a dog could hear.

Game after game of solitaire, and I haven't won one yet.
How many days is it? Tides come in, tides go out.

I stay inside, waiting out the statute of limitations,
off the grid, under an alias, kayak from cove to cove
as the families come and go like duck pods in the mist
that obliterates everything until it all returns again,
and the little shack at the end of the beach flies both
the American and the Canadian flags.

IV

Impressions, the vicious end of the cove, black rocks
and broken trees, tough green seaweed, muscles
and hard barnacles, everything picks a spot to survive.
No transmissions, cell tower silent on Mount Constitution,
I'm gathering firewood as a shadow tends the oyster garden,
sun low, shade lengthening, forest dipping limbs in the sea.

A seagull rises and drops a clam that shatters on a rock.
The gull descends and feeds, centuries of this design.
From here all you see are trees, not the shape of the land,
but if you run   then, through the gaps you see everything.

The oyster gardener bangs the sand from his traps,
a sound like a drum or the faltering of the earth's heart.
Warm sunlight, father and son by the edge of the water.
I was once both of them: little kid with a stick on the beach,
beating a rock, digging a hole, writing his name in the sand.

Wind braids the water's surface to impermanent cloud.
How many ways we misuse words like death and sunrise,
from what I've see through these narrow eyes.
Ragged sleeve of care, dark oblivion home everywhere,
smoke assembling and torn, and without even this
flicker of a doubt accept the moment you are born.

The innkeeper says in a split second a ghost stole her lunch
when she wasn't looking. The cleaning staff say it's Emma—
second from the right in that photograph by the bay window,
and from the shadow chair there on the west-facing deck
I leap up from the cold passing cloud of unknowing.

Pointing at the moon: when I am free and see the codes in air,
the ocean wave and maple tree, I also see the old self mind
like a drunk on the ground searching for his keys.

Enlightenment? The big wave crashes over the mountain.
I swim free of a boat you'd barely notice if I didn't mention it.
The last cherry blossom falls in my book: see it in the margin?
I carried a mind into the cove, into the water, the blue mirror sky,
the white pavilions of far-off sovereignties that emerge
then disappear—the mind forgets, but I remember.

V

I see a kid, a numbskull, jumping on a bed,
splitting his head open on the windowsill.
He slips out nights, wanders the neighborhoods
chasing alligators through the backyards.
He stands in a living room, late afternoon sunlight
splitting through the door glass and shimmering
like electric nerves splattered all over the ceiling,
and that's when I slip in, take over, and live his life.

This house is no longer my own, but I go to the porch
and see familiar things   my things: a notebook
and a chair. The people inside are dressed in black.
Someone has died. I go away. I live in another house
across the street next to a vacant lot. I hate this kitchen.

I drive off a cliff and believe my car is a plane. Falling,
I realize my mistake and dream myself back again.
I wake and wake, think: the woman of the rocks has
many names: ticket-taker at the turnstile, elevator operator,
the snake-haired smoker fixing you with a stone stare,
witch turning the contents of the cauldron, stirring sky
blood-boiling red with funnel and fury and crackling
dry lightning, nervous laughter lighting the city, lighting
the docks and the waves and the hidden stowaways
there on the ship that is just now arriving for thee...

She says she's a force of nature, but she's really just
death's little sister: one hundred pounds of might
and mayhem dancing by firelight, and I've been
cold long enough to slip into that hot slot of ash,
burning coals, my Lorelei, on liberty from the ship
far from the peaceful little cabin by the frozen river
where I bend to kiss the life-giving lips in the flames.

Alone with a lofty view across the oceans at night,
I float disembodied among the campfires of the dead.
Come morning I rise and look out over the sea waves
flowing in relentlessly and born out of nothing.
You might think it lonely, but it's not—I lived
in cities of irrational anger, intrigue, but now I'm free
and see the pyrotechnics, sparks and flares of fantasy.
I have no desire to go back, so I send you this signal,
warning: beware the rocks that'll wreck your ship.

The induction committee approved my nomination,
clean and simple. The not-so-famous but interesting
poet friend came to visit and slept in the basement.
Alarms going off, the woman asked, have you settled?
I wasn't sure if she meant the lawsuit or my life.
Head to the woods, it's good for your immune system.
She said she woke up from her life and is now
living in a past that constantly repeats itself, but I think
she got that from a book. In the apocalypse version of this,
movie theaters lie destroyed along with phones and TVs.
We're back to drinking from streams, hacking out shelter
in the woods, and at night when people gather by a big fire
to listen to the storyteller, they call it going to the movies.

I was cutting firewood, and I kept seeing little sparks
floating in the air. I realized this was happening under water,
but we all forgot what water was. Only then did I realize
how sluggishly my arms moved. It seemed amazing and almost
impossible that the axe head could cut through wood at all.
I believed I was creating miracles. Then body appears, bud-tip
first, the top of the head emerging blue with eyes clapped shut,
so I fly down and whisper the secret code into his ear
as the eyes open and he takes a breath and starts to wail.

I wake up in cloud consciousness reading your paper,
reading your tea leaves, wind rattling your windows,
blowing pollen over your fields, and I climb into a crow suit

and perch at the top of a sycamore tree to watch
the waves rolling endlessly. Call it voyeurism, call it love,
call it what you will as storyteller tells his story and we drift
in dreams of our own in the swaying current of night
beside low-glowing embers of a campfire light.

Disappearing

I don't mind disappearing for a lifetime or two.
Oh, great windy leap, no pain on concussion,
and nothing but a slow watery descent.

I don't mind disappearing into the wilderness,
to a squatter's shack on the river, the ice of winter,
and the shield of poplars swaying in the wind,

I don't mind disappearing. What was I anyway
beyond air, beyond stone, a bare-bone monk routine
of life-lurching urges, old verities, free but witnessing?

I don't mind disappearing. I've done it before,
as a welder, designated driver, one with bail money
and a sympathetic ear, a warm bed and a shelter.

I don't mind disappearing, art requiring nothing,
so take the coat, the books, the knack for invisibility,
willingness to surrender resistance to karmic swings.

I don't mind disappearing. I practice it a lot,
simply holding true to the true intent to stand
unmoving on the forest path to the spring.

I tell you I don't mind disappearing, it's a relief
from the onslaught of things, beautiful friends,
here for a moment, gone in a snap—I don't mind.
I don't mind disappearing. I do it   like   that.

Notes on *The Cabin at the End of the World*

"Block 23," the pairs of chromosomes in a human cell, common code "roots," physical and literary, a sort of can you spot it.

"A Game of Chicken," asked if this is "true"—the important parts are.

"Drive Through," Russ, a psychiatrist, one sleepless night.

"Pigeon Man," where the condition shows more acutely the effects.

"Noted for The Grey Man," to be continued.

"American Dharma," ironic wisdom. Nevertheless, here more explicitly themes arise related to the work of various Chinese masters, Cf. *Classical Chinese Poetry*, translated by David Hinton, the Rivers and Mountains poets, "Enlightenment as becoming the emptiness of absence," (ref Hsieh Ling-Yun, as well as the "exiled spirit moving through the world," (ref Li Po).

"Flowmatic," "Darren Aronofsky claims that any resemblance between *Requiem for a Dream* and *Perfect Blue* is an 'homage.'"

"The Messenger," Cf. *Community*.

"Lashed to the Mast," Cf. Bukowski lighting a cigarette, *Born into This*.

"Talking Stone," do you remember where you were during the pandemic?

"Distances," the tercet, a trinity of lines, 3-part god. "Tu Fu spent years wandering the outer fringes of the Chinese cultural sphere…a panoramic view of the human drama." (ref Tu Fu).

"Road of Bones," Cf. Siberia.

"Getting Yourself Home," Berkeley, CA, the year is a blur.

"Healing Rain," Cf. McCarthy, "The Judge."

"Chasing Tiger," Cf. Dillinger Steel, *Chasing Tiger*, or the previous incarnation, *China White*.

"Estrella," San Diego, Kensington Theater, Normal Heights.

"Dark Carnival," 40 min. walk from Virginia Street to Claremont Avenue.

"The Windows of the Sea," Cf. Bob Dylan, "Desolation Road," dreaming is no escape. Also, "Po Chu-I "Found himself exiled…quiet recluse poetry…" and Li Ho, "ghostly genius". "Li Ho spent his days wandering on the back of a donkey, and when a line came to him, he would scribble it down and toss it into a bag," (ref Li Ho).

"Disappearing," Cf. Elizabeth Bishop, "The Art of Losing." Losing, what?

"My dear friend nowhere in sight,
This Han River keeps flowing east.

Now, if I look for old masters here,
I find empty rivers and mountains."
            -Wu Wei

Acknowledgments

Earlier versions appeared in the following journals and anthologies:

Another Chicago Magazine, "Notes for the Grey Man"
Cathexis, "Another Universe,"
Bending Genres, "Casino People"
Black Coffee Review, "The Messenger"
Channel Magazine, "No SOS On" (Also a Video Poem)
Cider Press Review, "Dear Reader," and "Pointing at the Moon" (from "West Cove")
Dream Noir, "The Street of Lost Steps," "Pigeon Man"
Drunk Monkey, "The End of the World"
Dune, "The Couple in Room 416"
Fredericksburg Literary and Art Review "Cabin in the Darkness," "The Road No One Goes Down," (from "West Cove")
Goats Milk, "Into the Zone"
Great Weather for Media, "Drive Through"
Heartland Review, "Lonesome Driver" (Also a Video Poem)
Hole in the Head Review, "Distances" (Also a Video Poem),
North of Oxford, "Impressions" (from "West Cove")
Innisfree, "Night Prayer," "Talking to Yourself" (from "West Cove")
Maudlin House Magazine, "Drive Through"
Medusa's Kitchen, "Backwards Revolved the Luminous Wheel," "Dark Carnival"
MiGoZine, "Lashed to the Mast"
Night Heron Barks, "Four Way," "Revisiting Erskine Way," "Coming and Going Itself," "Pointing at the Moon," and "Re-entry"
The Penn Review "Flowmatic"
Penumbra, "Cartoon Moment"

Poetry South, "Lonesome Driver"

Plato's Cave, "Mind as Blank as a Room"

Punch Drunk Press, "Patrolman"

Rathalla, "Cartoon Moment"

Riggwelter, "Healing Rain"

Sandy River Review, "Getting Yourself Home," "Dead Center," "The Companion,"

Star 82 Review, "Circular Highway"

Setu Magazine, "Infinite Gaze," "Beauty of the World," "Widowmaker"

Sonic Boom, "Memento"

Sweet, "Caught in a Dream" (as "And That Dark") (Nominated Best of the Net)

Tipton Review, "Boethius Said," "Ivan"

Third Wednesday, "Road of Bones," "Winter Vision," "Tuesday's Purge"

Toyon Multilingual Journal of Literature, "On Broadway"

Twelve Mile Review, "Chasing Tiger"

Two Hawks Quarterly, "An Inside Job," "East Sounder" (from "West Cove")

Unlikely Stories, "Estrella"

Valparaiso, "Standing on the Water" (from "West Cove")

Washington Square Review, "Notes for the Grey Man"

Wisconsin Review, "A Game of Chicken," "Rolling the Bones"

Write Now, "Mind as Blank as a Room"

About the Author

Douglas Cole has published six poetry collections and the novel *The White Field*, winner of the American Fiction Award. His work has appeared in journals such as *Beloit Poetry, Fiction International, Valpariaso, The Gallway Review* and *Two Hawks Quarterly*; as well as anthologies such as *Bully* Anthology (Hopewell), *Bindweed* Anthology, and *Work* (Unleash Press). He contributes a regular column, "Trading Fours," to the magazine *Jerry Jazz Musician*; edits the selections of American writers for *Blue Citadel,* part of *Read Carpet* journal of international writing produced in Columbia. In addition to the American Fiction Award, his screenplay of *The White Field* won Best Unproduced Screenplay Award in the Elegant Film Festival, and he has been awarded the Leslie Hunt Memorial prize in poetry, the Best of Poetry Award from Clapboard House, First Prize in the "Picture Worth 500 Words" from *Tattoo Highway*, and the Editors' Choice Award in fiction by *RiverSedge*. He has been nominated six times for a Pushcart and seven times for Best of the Net. He lives and teaches in Seattle, Washington. His website is https://douglastcole.com/.

About the Press

Unsolicited Press is based out of Portland, Oregon and focuses on the works of the unsung and underrepresented. As a womxn-owned, all-volunteer small publisher that doesn't worry about profits as much as championing exceptional literature, we have the privilege of partnering with authors skirting the fringes of the lit world. We've worked with emerging and award-winning authors such as Shann Ray, Amy Shimshon-Santo, Brook Bhagat, Kris Amos, and John W. Bateman.

Learn more at unsolicitedpress.com. Find us on X (formerly Twitter) and Instagram.

R

Printed in the USA
CPSIA information can be obtained
at www.ICGtesting.com
JSHW081157071024
70788JS00006B/141